Unending MARITAL BLESSINGS

Dr. Harry Tobechi Nze

Author's Tranquility Press
MARIETTA, GEORGIA

Copyright © 2025 by Dr. Harry Tobechi Nze

All rights reserved. No part of this publication may be reproduced, distributed or transmitted in any form or by any means, including photocopying, recording, or other electronic or mechanical methods, without the prior written permission of the publisher, except in the case of brief quotations embodied in critical reviews and certain other noncommercial uses permitted by copyright law. For permission requests, write to the publisher, addressed "Attention: Permissions Coordinator," at the address below.

Dr. Harry Tobechi Nze/Author's Tranquility Press
531 Roselane Street NW Suite 400-175
Marietta, GA 30060
www.authorstranquilitypress.com

Ordering Information:
Quantity sales. Special discounts are available on quantity purchases by corporations, associations, and others. For details, contact the "Special Sales Department" at the address above.

Unending Marital Blessings / Dr. Harry Tobechi Nze
Hardback: 978-1-967776-11-5
Paperback: 978-1-965463-71-0
eBook: 978-1-965463-39-0

Contents

DEDICATION ....

CHAPTER 1 1

CHAPTER 2 16

CHAPTER 3 25

CHAPTER 4 35

CHAPTER 5 43

CHAPTER 6 53

CHAPTER 7 58

This book will turn your marital pressure into pleasure and your pleasure into a treasure.

DEDICATION

This book is dedicated to families that seek peace that passes all understand. Hope they get it. Without PEACE, there will be no family progress.

To my wife, Angelic Angela...thanks for standing beside me as I continue to function in the marriage/relationship gifting the Lord decorated us with. And I say to you that every woman is born a female but not all females are wives. And try as I did I could not dig out all the virtues of your womanhood. You successfully sustained virtue in your mission to my family - knitting all and sundry together. And I sought for a more pleasant words to thank you. I couldn't find. So permit me to fall back on the old reliable - THANK YOU!!!

To Prince and Chidebe, Chijioke and Tobechi Nze, thank you for being such friends. You are more than that. You all are my life. Thank you all for all we do together.

To my children - Tobechi, Kendy, Dindu. Ojk and Shallom:

Thank you all for being patient with me and your Mom. You have all proven right about training children the way they should go...

To my family at Victory Community Church. God sent us to meet each other and we have not only enjoyed fellowship but also followership.

Thanks to you:

Mosley and Christiana Ogbanga
Vincent Egevbru and family
Ikwuagwu Kalu Igwe and family
Toby and Tina Toby and family

CHAPTER 1

Embracing the V-Word: Vision

What Is Vision?

Let me begin by laying a foundation around the key word vision. God has a grand plan for His children. He has a plan for each of us:

> For I know the thoughts that I think toward you, saith the LORD, thoughts of peace, and not of evil, to give you an expected end. (Jeremiah 29:11)

You are not created to roam about in life. You are designed for a specific purpose. He knew you before you were born, and He separated you for a specific goal and assignment.

It is very important to know that your placement in the master plan of God is located by *vision*. Vision is a pathfinder. It is the pathfinding tool in the hand of everyone born of a woman. Joel 2:28 says, "your young men shall see visions." At age seventy-five, Abraham had a vision. In the sight of God, you are a young man even at seventy-five!

- ✓ Vision is the mental picture of the future.
- ✓ It is the unfolding of a divine plan as it relates to

individuals.
- ✓ It is a supernatural insight into one's purpose for existence.
- ✓ Vision is a necessary and indispensable tool or ingredient in the process of achievement in life and ministry.

Some Facts about Vision

- ➢ Vision provides access into the divine program for an individual.
- ➢ It is the basis or foundation upon which a successful framework is built
- ➢ All feats of valor begin and are sustained by vision.
- ➢ Vision drives its owner beyond the limits.
- ➢ It is a spiritual cord that draws water from the deep well of life.

The Bible says, "Where there is no vision, the people perish." This is true about marriage. Where there is no vision, marriages perish. Vision is a principal factor in actualizing any dream. The marriage dream will fall like a pack of cards without this virtue called vision. It is a firm foundation upon which good marriages thrive.

Planning is an integral part of vision. The word *plan* means "a set of intended actions, usually mutually related, through which one expects to achieve a goal." It is a set of programs toward a specific goal. It is an action graph, an arrangement of carefully drawn out steps one must follow in order to fulfill an ultimate desire.

To fail to plan is already a plan to fail. Great people are astute planners. They succeed before they begin by putting up excellent plans and action procedures.

The greatest example of an excellent planner is God. God is a God of plan and action. There are certain steps involved in God's achievements:

1. God verbalizes His plan.
2. He articulates it.
3. He executes it.
4. He designates responsibilities.

In Genesis 1:1, the Almighty God initiated the vision to create the heaven and the earth as primary on His to-do list. He called a board meeting of Father, Son, and Holy Spirit. The vision was clearly spelled out, and responsibilities were carried out by each member of the Trinity. The three board members were abreast of the vision; they were all on the same page, and each performed the responsibilities leading to actual fulfillment of the vision.

> The *Son* was the word that cleared the darkness. Read this:
>
> In the beginning God created the heaven and the earth.
>
> And the earth was without form and void, and darkness
>
> Was upon the face of the deep. And the Spirit of God moved
>
> Upon the face of the deep. (Genesis 1:1)
>
> In the beginning was the word, and the word was with God, And the word was God.
>
> The same was in the beginning with God.
>
> And all things were made by Him and without Him was not anything Made that was made.
>
> And the light shineth in darkness and the darkness comprehended it not.
>
> (John 1:1)

On His part, God the Holy Spirit brought back peace and

tranquility that created a continual link in creation: "… and the Spirit of God moved upon the face of the deep." And Adam was designated to tend and nurture the garden.

Vision is very important in all spheres of life. God never does anything without a clear definition of what He wants to achieve. In Luke 1, He defined what kind of child John the Baptist would be. He went ahead to design his job description.

> and you will have joy and many will rejoice at his 15. for he shall be great before the sight of The Lord, and shall drink neither wine nor strong drink, He will also Be filled with the Holy Spirit even from the mother's womb, 16. And He will turn many of the children of Israel to the Lord their God, 17, He Will also go before Him in the spirit and power of Elijah, to turn the hearts of the fathers to the children, and the disobedient to the wisdom Of the just, to make ready a people prepared for the Lord. (Luke 1:14–17 NKJV)

And as we read down to verses 28–34, we see God introducing and verbalizing the vision of the birth of our Lord, Jesus Christ, to his earthly mom, Mary.

> And having come in, the angel said to her, "rejoice, highly favored one, the Lord is with you; blessed are you among women!"

> Verse 31:

> and behold, You will conceive in your womb and bring forth a son, and shall call His name, Jesus … He will be great, and will be called the son of the Highest; and the Lord God will reign over the house of Jacob forever and of His kingdom there will be no end. (NKJV)

We can clearly see from the scripture that God initiated the plan of the birth of our Lord and Savior, Jesus Christ. Having verbalized it, He went ahead with His action plans and included certain agents that would be part of the vision. The Angel of the Lord came with the message. Mary was in the equation. Later on, we see the passive role of Joseph. This is a typical example of vision and planning.

What Is the Vision of Your Marriage to Your Spouse?

This is a very important question every spouse must ask himself or herself. Love contacts and introduces marriage, but in the long run, it is vision that sustains marriage. "Without vision the people perish." Unequivocally, without vision, the marriages will perish! Any marriage without vision is hanging on a loose platform of endurance and possible disintegration.

How wonderful it would be for "friends" who want to get married to sit down and have a lengthy discussion about what their marriage would look like forever.

Do you want to marry? Why do you want to marry? When do you want to marry? Who do you want to marry? How do you want to marry? Where do you want to marry? Do you want to have children? How long do you want to remain married? What are you prepared to bring to the table? How would you make your marriage work? Do you have knowledge for everlasting marriage? These and other pertinent questions should flood your finite mind before you tie the nuptial cord.

The Honey and the Moon

Vision will ensure that this relationship is first in godly order and must be guided by guidelines outlined in God's book of life. The

Bible is God's manual of life for us. Yes, because it contains the 4 Ps of life, namely; PROPHECY, PROMISES, PROVISIONS, PRAYERS, and PERSUASION.

Manufacturers include a manual of operation with their machines or devices. The manual is a guide on the use of the equipment. Failure to adhere strictly to the instructions in the manual may lead to malfunctioning of the device. In some cases, the device may fail to respond or perform to optimal capacity.

The Bible is the manual of life. It is God's handout to guide our lives, including the marriage institution. It is the Christian's charter, the soldier's sword, the pilot's compass, and the pilgrim's staff. Let us consider the following acronym:

B: Basic

I: Instruction

B: Before

L: Living

E: Earth

The Bible contains all required basic instructions vital for success in life— marriage, ministry, business, and so forth. It is our manual of life. It contains our modus operandi.

Marriage is not a short-haul contract. It is a long haul, a lifetime journey. Intending couples must seek knowledge for everlasting marriage by establishing a viable and godly vision. The time of vision sharing is the best quality time any couple can ever have. People should not go on a honeymoon to watch the moon. Couples who go on a honeymoon should return with honey in their mouths, having reviewed and consolidated the vision for their marriage.

Many years ago, I and my wife verbalized this statement over our union: "we shall bring up our children in a godly manner until we watch them bring up their own children in a godly manner." Many years have come and gone, and this vision is still fresh in the hearts of each person. Sometimes vision is the foundation upon which love exists, just as hope is the substance upon which faith operates. There are times in later years when love begins to wane, but vision will not let love perish. It will continue to provide its shoulders for the marriage to hang on until love bounces back.

Bill and Hillary Clinton

I watched the trillion-dollar smile on the face of Hillary Clinton on the day their only daughter, Chelsea, was wed. There he was, Bill Clinton, with Chelsea on his arm, walking the aisle to hand Chelsea over to Mark. Sometimes things happen, and love begins to fade. At that point, vision sets in to hold the fort until love springs back. What broke and disintegrated millions of marriages in the United States of America was a nonissue to Hillary Clinton. We all know the story. I saw vision in the eyes of Hillary, confirming the understanding that love contacts and confirms marriage, but vision sustains marriage.

Like Canaan

Like Canaan (the land of milk and honey), different unexpected experiences should not stop the march to the next wedding anniversary, when the vision of the marriage will be reviewed and rededication of the marriage between the two verbalized. Age and time do two things. Either they integrate the union more or it gradually disintegrates the relationship.

The days of President Bill Clinton's trial for infidelity presented an opportunity for a lesser wife to file for divorce and clear the family finances. No! Not a wife of the caliber of Hillary. It is possible to think that she stuck to Bill because she had a political ambition, which was expressed in 2008 when she contested presidency of the United States. Yet I do not think it is wrong to envision that the central figure of the vision of the marriage between Bill and Hillary was Chelsea, their only daughter.

Hillary did what many American women would not do; she relinquished money for vision until she watched Bill Clinton, her husband and father of Chelsea, honor Chelsea and Mark as the father of the bride. They have remained married ever after. *Self* makes spouses separate from each other, unmindful of the children. But the days are coming, the Bible reminds us, a time when a set of children will be born and their primary objective will be to "Turn the hearts of fathers to their children." (Luke 1:17 KJV)

Brother Emma and Sister Chinyere-Emma Okorie

Brother Emma Okorie is the president and apostle of Living Word Ministries.

He is married to his ageless wife, Chinyere-Emma Okorie. As young Christians, they understood that love *contacts*, *attracts,* and *contracts* marriage, but vision sustains marriage.

So they took time to discern the heartbeat of God and the enormity of the work of the ministry God had revealed to them individually before falling into each other's arms in marriage. Once together and now filled with the Holy Spirit, they have since centered their lives and marriage on *"making His will be done on earth as it is done in heaven."* The product of that visionary union is seen in the Kingdom of God. Their ministry is rife with open doors and breakthroughs in the lives of people. Testimonies of their impact abound. Souls are convicted, convinced, and converted. People are adequately counseled. They find joy in the Holy Spirit and are comforted by the words they speak and prayers they make. The sick are healed, and those that are confused find direction. Praise the Lord! Starting from Samaria (Nigeria), they are overtaking Jerusalem (the world) with a training center for practical application of the Bible, a notable and popular Christian hospital, Christian schools all over Nigeria and the western coasts of Africa, churches and ministries all over the world, and, last but not least, Rhema Christian University. Love has not faded, yet vision keeps knitting husband and wife together.

Do they have personal and private issues and challenges in their marriage? They answered "Yes!" in a crowded marriage-counseling season. "Despite the fact that we could not reach agreement on a very touchy issue, we went to bed with an attitude to each other—you know, kind of facing the other way. But it did not stop my wife, Chinyere, from doing her duty of covering me up with a blanket when the weather turned windy and chilly."

Continuing, Brother Emma revealed, "With one eye open, I mused to myself, *So you still care, even when we are having 'attitude.'*" Vision is the engine room of forgiveness. It makes spouses live above pettiness in marriage.

Phillip and Brenda Goudeaux

We met Dr. Phillip and Brenda Goudeaux, pastors of Calvary Christian Center, Sacramento, presidents and founders of Fellowship of Covenant Ministers International, in 2001. As often as every Sunday, Dr. Goudeaux would challenge his members with his marriage to his lovely wife, Brenda. When love brought them closer, they saw beyond love and discerned vision. Pastor Goudeaux was so proud of his marriage that he would stand on the podium and challenge ladies to tell on him if he had messed with any since he got married. Such was the frankness and integrity that surrounded his boldness that I and my wife decided to submit our ministry to his in the United States.

Today the ministry of Phillip and Brenda Goudeaux has continued to make disciples of Christ worldwide from their California base. Their recent breakthrough is the FCMI University.

Vision: Contending with and Blotting Out the Di-Prefix

In creation, God had a vision. His vision was to create, in six days, heaven and earth that was not only good but very good. The couple that would occupy this very good creation would not only be good but also be blessed.

They would occupy a geographical environment (housing); they got married (marriage) without the hassles that go with it, such as hiring a limo, renting a tuxedo and hall, choosing music, equipping their home, and so forth. They ate ready-made organic food and had a garden to relax in.

They were not in a recession and therefore had a job—to tend the garden. Everything that pertains to life and godliness was provided in excess. They lived in an atmosphere of peace and tranquility—the nature of heaven. Ultimately, they became the completion of the vision of the Almighty God for heaven and earth.

But who offended them that they added the prefix *di-* to the word *vision* of God? From that one act of Adam and Eve, the act of including the prefix *di*, everything went topsy-turvy. The prefix altered God's obedience to man's disobedience. The prefix *di* altered God's vision to man's division. The prefix *di-* altered God's ease to man's *disease*. It mutilated God's health to man's death. It reduced God's stable garden to man's destabilized world. With the inclusion of this demonic prefix, the world is bedeviled today with deceit, derision, destruction, dissension, disunity, dejection. With this demonic prefix *di*, the world is inundated with cases of murder, rebellion, immorality, betrayal, and all manner of sins.

This sin-soaked, degenerate, and depraved globe is the aftermath of a demonic prefix.

Incidentally, the one disobedient spirit that destroyed the peace of heaven is still destroying the peace of households and marriages, still destroying the peace of offices, churches, communities, businesses, and investments. One divisive spirit will destroy the peace of anything. Anything! Once disobedience succeeds in destabilizing the peace of a home, the house will be engaged in war.

War of Words

We live in a world of words and corresponding actions. All human relationships are fostered by words and corresponding actions. All human achievements are governed by words and resultant actions. Wherever we are, whatever we do or want to achieve, words and corresponding actions are indispensable. People fight after vituperative outpourings of pent-up emotions. Nations go to war after words are spoken to vent the feelings of each warring party.

The base, or the armory, for marital destruction is the mouth. I have fought and won all kinds of wars, but when it comes to the arena and battlefield of the war of words, I am in a hurry to give up my rights. Words from the mouth are either destructive or constructive, because inside the mouth is hidden a most lethal weapon, which has destroyed millions of marriages, rendered many homeless, caused children to be parented by televisions and caregivers in group and juvenile homes. That weapon is called "the tongue". It is a WMD: weapon of mass destruction.

The tongue hides like a serpent or scorpion inside the mouth and spits out poisonous words: words that cannot be recovered, corrected, or amended once they hit the ear of the receiver. Like the poison spit by the serpent or the strike of the scorpion, words from the tongue never return to the sender void. It must accomplish the evil for which it is sent. It will either hurt or halt.

Here lies our authority and power to conquer the tongue.

> Behold I give you the authority to trample upon serpents and scorpions
>
> And over all the powers of the enemy and nothing shall any means hurt you. (Luke 10:19)
>
> Death and life are in the power of the tongue. (Proverbs 18: 21)

The capacity and capability of the tongue to build or to destroy can be discerned from the word *power* that is always used to qualify *tongue*. It has the power to heal or to destroy.

But the good news is that the power of the tongue can be controlled by the power that lies within us. That power within us can ply the tongue to wherever we want.

With the tongue, the serpent hoodwinked the woman, and with the tongue the woman added the prefix *di-* to the vision of God, deceiving the man and creating permanent division and disunity on earth.

Spouses who use words negatively and indiscriminately should expect discord and division in the household. Such a negative attitude is the seed of the devil. The devil is evil. If you add a *d* to *evil*, what you get is *devil*. He is the household wickedness we must chase out by being positive in our confessions. Shun anger. *Anger* is one letter short of *danger*.

After God created the earth and qualified it as good, He did not give anybody power to refer to what is good as bad. No spouse has the right to speak to the other in a negative language. To do so is to challenge God's opinion of what He has approved as good. God does not take this kind of attitude lightly. God did not find

Miriam's tongue-lashing of Moses in the book of Numbers funny.

No one wonders that He dealt with Miriam harshly. Check this out.

> And Miriam was shut out of the camp seven days, and the people journeyed not until Miriam was brought in again. (Numbers 12:15)

What the heck! Because of bad and foul language, Miriam was struck with leprosy and quarantined for several days! Imagine what retrogressive harm bad words are causing in homes and households.

The striking truth here is that the camp did not move for seven days. When spouses make quarrels, bad words, and irresponsible outbursts a habit in marriage, they quarantine love, peace, and good cohabitation. The marriage soon becomes leprous. The relationship can break down irredeemably

From seven days to seven weeks, seven months, seven years— within that period, everything in the household, including the children, begins to suffer. Love in the marriage begins to dwindle, and eventually there is a fall. Every fall has a beginning. (Matthew 14: 22–23)

> It must needs that offenses shall come but woe unto that man through whom offenses cometh. (Matthew 18:7)

Most Christian marriages are battling with woes that spouses brought upon themselves through irresponsible use of the tongue.

Taming the Tongue

Most therapists, psychologists, and other "ists" ask the couple to separate from each other when offense is triggered. Some Bible scholars counsel self-control, as a fruit of the Spirit should "take control of anger." But the Lord has revealed the most appropriate step to take.

> Therefore a man shall leave his father and mother and be joined by his wife and they shall become one flesh. (Genesis 2:24)

This scripture confirms the teaching that God is the author of marriage. Just as God got up with a to-do list to create the heaven and the earth, we can also safely say that at a major spreadsheet was His program to create marriage. And He created marriage. When we backtrack to the beginning in Genesis 1:1–2, we could metaphorically say, "In the beginning, God created marriage. But without God, marriages are formless and empty, pervaded by darkness, cheating, accusations, sins (vanity upon vanity)."

I believe what we need is the Spirit of God to hover over marriages and birth them into God's Light. The lesson is simple. Only the Holy Spirit can bring peace when darkness overtakes a hitherto good marriage.

Over the years, I have counseled couples that whenever they are triggered by the impulse to speak destructive language to their spouse, they should be sensitive enough to stop a while and count to seven. That allows the Holy Spirit to hover upon their mouths and tread upon their tongues and keep them in check over the words they want to utter. And it works. Couples have found this useful in blotting out the *di* that threatens the "vision" of their marriages.

Secret Number One

Have vision for your marriage, or you will be battling with the *di-*

prefix in *vision*: di-vision. Under extreme provocation, please allow the Holy Spirit to hover over your mouth and tread upon your tongue. If you do, whatever you utter will be good, very good, as it was in the beginning.

CHAPTER 2

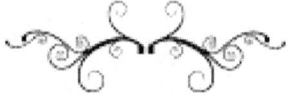

Invite the Author to Finish

The altar is a place of invitation. The altar is a place of exchange. It is a place of surrender—absolute surrender to the will, way, and word of God. We present our old life and return to our seat with the new. The altar is a place of blood transfusion. We voluntarily present our natural blood in exchange for the supernatural blood of the lamb. It is divine mystery, and that's why it is unseen and mysterious. Yet to those who believe, it is the power of God unto salvation. It happens in seconds, but the reward is everlasting. Yet it starts with presenting ourselves voluntarily at the altar in response and answer to a call.

In John chapter 2, we see the uncommon sense in the invitation extended to our Lord Jesus Christ to the wedding in Cana of Galilee. Just as the wine that came from a touch of the Lord became the best, so will life in Him also be the best. So why do couples wait for relationships to turn sour before inviting the king of kings? Why wait to have the best at last, when the best is around the corner, wishing to be invited to introduce new wine into your old issues and challenges.

Christian couples should not take the wedding home, leaving the marriage at the altar. They must build an altar of remembrance for the Lord in their homes if they wish to relish in their new wine every day of their lives as lovers. Couples who invite the Lord Jesus Christ and steady Him in their marriages will experience (sorry, enjoy) the re-creation and reformation that is associated with His miraculous works.

There is no better time for couples to invite the Lord Jesus into their married lives than now, when world affairs are chaotic. The economy is going bananas. The center of relationships can no longer hold.

People are loving what God hates. Divorce has become the hobby of many, and spouses are becoming homeless. Televisions are playing more roles in parenting than parents. This situation is likened to what was in existence in Genesis 1:1 before the Spirit of God moved upon the waters, creating peace and tranquility.

Homes are as "formless" as the earth was in the beginning. Spouses are void of love. Darkness has overtaken the deep of marriages, and children have gone haywire, making common of holy things. Children no longer have family virtues and values. Family values and honor are supposed to be inculcated into children by parents, and the children in turn evangelize their peer groups with what they know or obtained from their homes.

If the Spirit of God does not brood over the waters of families, bringing back peace, love, and tranquility; divorce rates will escalate and world family systems will continue to crash. The aftermath will be more divorce, youthful amorous adventures, and all kinds of vices.

The good news is that as Christ was in heaven during those days of formlessness and darkness, waiting to produce the light that will swallow up darkness, so He is still at the doorsteps of families, knocking and waiting to be invited to add strength to every weak area of our marriages.

So what? So spouses! Take a sacrificial step today and invite the Prince of Peace into your marriage, into your family and homes, and He will redecorate your relationships with *peace*—and not ordinary peace, but peace *that passeth all understanding,* an open door to all-round success.

Nothing can be achieved in a household without peace! Therefore, invite him now. Inviting our Lord Jesus Christ into your marriage is not like driving through MacDonald's in search of your favorite burger or parking at Burger King for a bite of your usual. No! No! The benefit of this invitation can only be derived when we are determined to obey and do things His way without questioning His authority. We must be prepared to obey His principle as outlined in the manual of life: the Bible.

His Invitation Is a Game Changer

Every ball game has a game changer. The coach knows when to place his priced game changer to achieve victory for his team. What the opposing team does is prevent the ball from getting to the game changer, in the same way the devil stops spouses from getting to their Jesus.

In soccer, it is the midfielder (David Beckham). In basketball, it is the point guard (Derek Fisher). In football, it is the quarterback (Tom Brady), and in baseball, it is the pitcher (Alex Rodriguez). These outstanding gentlemen are breathlessly marked in their respective games simply because they possess a quality or qualities that will change the game and bring victory to their team.

The same goes for marriages. The enemy of our faith in the Lord fights to stop us from seeing the wonderful qualities in our spouses that bring joy and eternal peace to God and humankind. When spouses open their inner eyes, they will see that what the enemy is actually contesting is the wonderful quality in store in the lives of each other. Also, the enemy plants jealousy in order to prevent God from reaping the harvest of godly children from a union He Himself put together. Children are the targets of separation or divorce. Spouses, open your eyes and see. Do not have open eyes that do not see. Jesus is the positive game changer of our lives and marriages. He is the author of marriage. When He is invited, He will finish what He began to author, for in all situations He knows what to do. (John 6:6)

New Wine for the Old

Back to John 2: the bride and her groom had made a perfectly finished plan of what would in popular media clichés be termed *wedding of the year*. There was excitement in the air, and booze was moving everywhere. The decorations on the long robes were as various as the diversity of titles attached to the names of personalities present. In Africa, kings and priests will send their assistants to ensure that none of their long titles is left behind as their reverenced presence is announced.

But the scenario in John 2 is not African stuff. It is Jewish. And the Jews celebrate weddings for upwards of six days. The mother of Jesus was there. Jesus honored their invitation. Culturally, Jews consider it an embarrassment when a wedding invitation is rejected. No wonder weddings are usually held in places as big as a stadium.

Somewhere by the side of the hall lay the instrument to be used to restore order to the unforeseen challenges brewing in the air, in the background and behind the scenes: the finishing of the wine!

The six jars that were to be filled with water were there, but nobody knew their worth. And nobody cared. Jesus Christ, the Prince of Peace, is so close to helping us, but we ignore him and continue to see the devourer in each other.

Receive to Rededicate

As we get older in marriage, we should occasionally step aside to renew and rededicate our marriages; I mean to *re-receive* ourselves, if you like. The cup of water that was taken to the chairman of the occasion was still water in the hand of the cupbearer until the chairman received it. The principle is simple: what and whom we do not receive cannot make a change in our lives. Like salvation that generates instantaneous blood transfusion from the natural blood to the blood of the lamb, the water changed to wine as it was received. Some of the changes we made in our lives and ministry were a result of what we received from visiting ministers we hosted in our homes. What or whom you do not receive cannot make a change or reform your life. Invite the Lord to change the wine of your marriage so you can receive each other anew.

Separation and Divorce

Separation and divorce in marriage are like many things that started beautifully, only to turn sour along the line. The greatest examples of things that later turned sour are usually associated with human beings. As it is in marriage, so it is in business, relationships, schools, business, and—wait for it—churches! So when the wine was finished, the presence of the Lord made all the difference. New wine was brought. It amazes me why spouses delay bringing new wine to their relationships through making peace with the Prince of Peace and the Lord of Lords. Miracles are the nature of our Lord Jesus Christ. It is much more difficult to lay on hands and heal the sick or stretch out and lift the lame or even spit on the floor to open the eyes. In the case of marriage, it is easy for spouses to live in peace forever when they let in the Lord Jesus Christ, who, from the control room of the throne of the most High, will simply adjust the hearts of both spouses, provided they desire and earnestly covet and contend for peace through reconciliation.

Patience and Perseverance: John 5

Most spouses (especially women) only realize the hassles of divorce when they have deepened themselves into it. In 2004, I was privileged to speak to a group of career women of the Covenant Sisters Fellowship at Los Angeles. My topic was "Better Reunite Than Remarry." At the end of my session, I hosted two registered nurses who sneaked back from the crowd to say to me, "Pastor Harry, If I knew one quarter of what you said "Today", four years ago... I would still be in my marriage today."

Unfortunately, three things make it difficult to change minds and seek a reunification. The first is hypocritical Christian living (no knowledge of the scripture). The second is pride and career, and last, but not least, are greed and self. Naturally, they resist turning back and allow hostility to turn to hatred. Hatred, from my experience in years of counseling both in Africa and the United States, is the enemy's last joker in marital destruction. For when love turns to hatred, it hates with the same venom with which it loved. Spouses should think twice, even thrice, before pressuring themselves into divorce. Divorce is a selfish venture—selfish for him or her, and it certainly endangers the children.

Recently Katie Holmes, wife of Tom Cruise of *Mission Impossible* fame, filed divorce proceedings on Tom. She certainly had her personal reasons for that decision. However, from the outside, everybody thought that Suri, their only daughter, would be lured by mother's love to take Katie's side. Two things come into contention when hostility overtakes hospitality in marital relationships: child support and child custody, the latter being the most crucial. But little Suri decided it all.

"I want to stay with my daddy" was the shocking, shouting headline in all the major entertainment journals in the United States of America. What if Katie's decision to seek divorce had self and Suri in the background; you can see how Suri turned the table. Divorce leaves divorcees with too many uncertainties. Katie was shocked when Suri preferred Tom. Neither did Kim Kardashian anticipate that she would have Chris to contend with in order to be with Kanye West after their seventy-two-day old marriage.

A friend, in explaining why he is still single, said that folks wed on the balcony and move to the living room to print out divorce forms from the computer.

Marriage Is Hard Work; We Work Hard to Rest Hard

Yes, hard work, because it is the first part of God's divine creation power that He handed over to man. God worked hard to earn his rest on the seventh day. Out of His hard work He created everything that has become the raw material for the world's inventions. Human beings have never succeeded in creating anything. We are gurus in inventing and manufacturing from what God created.

But to enjoy rest we must work hard to earn and sustain the love of our spouses. We don't take ourselves for granted when we are joined together in matrimony.

Mantle of Peace and Enjoyment

There is a mantle of peace, love, and godliness to obtain if we have to enjoy and not endure marriage with our spouse. Like Elisha, we must make up our minds to follow each other in this journey for the mantle of peace, love, and godliness. We must be prepared to cross Galilee, Jericho, and the Jordan before we can expect the mantle. Oh dear, we must be ready to make a long haul, from Mount Sinai through Mount Cavalry and then at last to Mount Olive, if the mantle of peace, love, and godliness will drop in our laps.

Elisha worked hard with Elijah. All spouses are also expected to jointly work hard for each other's love and attention. If you lose the anointing to sleep on your spouse's lap, you will end up sleeping on Delilah's lap. Mark this: no one sleeps on Delilah's lap and wakes up in Abraham's bosom. Peace, love, and godliness usually quickly evaporates from the Bunsen burner (Delilah's lap), leaving a residue or scum of inversely proportional vices: war, hate, and unrighteous actions.

Hear what Elijah told Elisha: "You have asked a hard thing (literally: Boy! You have worked hard for what you want). Nevertheless, if you see me taken away (literally: if you work a little harder), you will receive what you asked for." Yet Elisha patiently persevered and exceeded the point of Nevertheless. I tell spouses who rage and race toward separation and divorce to venture to exceed the point of Nevertheless; they will suddenly receive fresh wine and a gold-plated mantle in their relationship with their spouses.

Foresight and knowledge of Jesus.

If all spouses who desire divorce and separation realize that our Lord Jesus saw and knew the state and condition of the man in the pool of Bethsaida before healing him, they would patiently persevere, believing that the healer heals. For whenever the water is troubled, there is a healing follow-up. When our day of healing comes, we do not have to know the correct answers to "Would you be made whole?" No! No! Healing is right there, waiting on His to-do list. How we answer will *not* deter or deny the healing that is in the locker for us. God did not bring us together to fail. He brought us out and joined us together in this marvelous relationship to take us to the Promised Land. He did not promise that there would be no giants on the land. No! He didn't. But one thing is certain:

> Call unto me and I will answer thee and show thee great and mighty things which thou knowest not. (Jeremiah 33:3)

And concerning the things He promised, He gave us an open check to *"Command ye me."* He will simply yank away the challenges that hinder peace in our marriages. Spouses are therefore expected to wear the breastplate of patience and perseverance. The instrument for healing is as close as the rod of Moses. Moses did not know the efficacy and power of the rod until he was told. Take my advice, and let the game changer change the negative state of your marriage to better and best, simply by inviting Him. As unnoticed as the jars in the obscure corner of the wedding hall were, yet those were the instruments positioned for miracles. Your own instrument was in position even before both of you began dating. That instrument is the Lord Jesus. He is right now as available to your family as ever. *Invite him now*!

Secret Two: You cannot finish a book you do not author. Therefore, spouses should invite the author to reveal the finishing part two of their book on marriage that everlasting peace will rule and reign.

CHAPTER 3

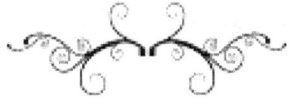

The Three Ws of Marriage

(My Hollywood Experience)

My understanding of the word "Where?" in the Bible is a call for accountability.

"Adam! Where are you?"

"Abraham, where is your wife, Sarah?"

"Cain, where is Abel thy brother?"

"Woman," Jesus asked, "where is your husband? Go call your husband." Here is the breaking news about the three *W*s of marriage.

It is not only a call for accountability but God's affirmation that He was and still is conscious and alert to matching spouses together as husband and wife. His action of posting a specific wife to a specific husband was deliberate. He brought couples together with full knowledge of their areas of weakness as their primary assignment to each other. God knows the name of that wife He posted to each husband. Conversely, He also knows the name of the husband married to any woman. And just like God went in the thick of the evening to see how Adam was doing with Eve; just as He appeared to Abraham at Mamre to ask for Sarah by name; just as our Lord had foreknowledge of the domestic circumstance of the woman of Samaria in John chapter 4, so He also knows the name of the husband He bonded any wife with.

On the last day, God will ask for an account of the love of the persons He gave us in trust to keep and to love on His behalf. For every man or woman is holding the love of his wife or husband in trust and in custody for the owner: the Almighty God!

My Hollywood Experience

From where we lived in Inglewood, California, I usually drove my wife to work at Westwood. This entailed driving through Wilshire Boulevard, a major route that links all major roads in Hollywood. That day, I saw a man and his family, one wife and four children, holding hands in a straight line as they crossed into the nearby movie theatre. There was a long line of almost one mile. The gentleman and his family joined the end of the line.

Somehow, I decided to park and watch. They got to the gate, and the man stood tall and handed over one ticket each to his wife, next his son, and so on until they were admitted into the theatre. The Spirit of the Lord witnessed that this is how it is going to be on the last day. Every man will be called to give account of the wife and family God brought to him.

Like managers who manage buildings and apartments on behalf of the owners, so we all, as custodians of the life and love of our wives and children, will be called upon to give account of them. A day shall come when the Almighty God will, in the cool of the evening (like in the days of Adam and Eve), come up with the W question.

> For we must all appear before the Judgment seat of Christ for each may receive what is due Him for the things done while in the body whether good or bad. (2 Corinthians 5:10 NIV)

God is mindful of us. His mind is full of us. He thinks of us every day. He has your details in the palms of His hands. He knows your name, middle name, and surname. He knows your house, office, and e-mail address. He knows your Twitter handle, BB pin, WhatsApp number, and all your social connections. He knows your weight, height, eye color, hobbies, likes and dislikes. He knows everything about you!

Do not be a fool in thinking that God does not know the name of your wife. It is foolhardiness to think that God does not know the name of your first husband. God, for the first time in the Ws of marriage, was teaching man family accountability. In this deal, ex-this or ex-that is not in the bargain. Any wonder the Bible did not mince words when it recorded these words: "I hate divorce!" says the Lord God of Israel. (Malachi 2:16 NIV)

Now we see that God did not make provisions for a second marriage. He only made strong provision for reconciliation in marriage, just as He made provisions for our reconciliation with Christ through salvation. This is why spouses are strongly advised to invite the Lord Jesus to their matrimonial homes in order to enjoy the benefits of His *five-fold reconciliation* ministry. Please read this:

> Consequently, from now on we estimate and regard no one from a (purely) human point of view (in terms of natural standards of value). (NO) even though we once did estimate Christ from a natural viewpoint and as a man, yet now (we have such knowledge of Him that) we know Him no longer in terms of flesh. (2 Corinthians 5:16 AMP)

A Christ-centered matrimonial relationship is supposed to be a replication and a reenactment of the act of spouses knowing each other *no longer in terms of flesh*: an attitude that lays the foundation for reconciliation at all times.

Verse 17: Therefore, if any person is (ingratiated) in Christ (the Messiah), he is a new creature (a new creature altogether); the old (previous moral and spiritual) has passed away. Behold the *fresh and new has come!*

A Christ-centered matrimonial relationship is supposed to trash the old (previous moral and spiritual) worldly ways of living while opening ways for *fresh and new* ways. And like salvation, reconciliation is the bedrock of fresh and new ways.

Verse 18: But all things are from God who through Jesus Christ reconciled (*) us to Himself (received us into favor, brought us into harmony with Himself) and gave to us the ministry of reconciliation (*), (that by word or deed we might aim to bring others into harmony with Him).

Verse 19: It was God (personally present) in Christ reconciling (*) and restoring the world to Himself, not counting up and holding against (men) their trespasses *(but canceling them)* and committing to us the message (ministry) of reconciliation (*) (of the restoration to favor).

Verse 20: So we are Christ's ambassadors; God making His appeal as it were through us (we as Christ's personal representatives) beg you for His sake to lay hold of His divine favor (now offered you) and be reconciled (*) to God.

The asterisks (*) depict the five-fold reconciliatory ministry provision made by God for spouses, which when appropriately applied should be an antidote against issues and challenges that lead to divorce.

The Bible tells us that "love covers a multitude of sins." In my opinion, divorce uncovers a magnitude of sins. Even when the common "unforgiveable?" sin of "he cheated on me" or "she cheated on me" (crises that spouses create for themselves by refusing to invite Christ to the marriages) surreptitiously creeps in to destroy and hurt marriages, the first thing couples think of is self before children. At the end of the day, they release each other to the Cheaters' Club where they (sometimes) remain as members ever after, while the children remain the cheated. The children remain lost in the hands of nonparents (in group and juvenile homes) whose level of care is quantified by the amount of the paycheck offered.

My Experience with Ursula

Ursula was three months into a separation heading toward divorce with Ted, her husband. Her reason for the separation was obvious: "He cheated on me!"

"How did you find out?"

"He told me. He confessed to me!"

"Good! So you forgave him, right?"

"No! You can't cheat on me and expect forgiveness!"

"So what did you do?"

"Simple. I moved out!"

"Oh. I thought he was the guy I saw you with in church last Sunday. Who is that?"

"Oh, that? He's Gabby. I met Gabby three days after I went to Tucson. He's awesome!"

"So?"

"So we're dating!"

"In other words, you released Ted to the Cheaters' Club and joined one yourself."

"What do you mean?"

"You have children?" I interjected.

"Yes, one boy, one girl. They are with his parents."

"Okay, Ursula. Would you want me to tell you the truth?"

"Of course, yes!"

I tried as modestly as I could to let her realize that at twenty-four, she still has many more years to live either alone or lonely with unwanted intruders, either enduring or enjoying the waves tossing to and from (lesser males than her husband), which is synonymous with the wilderness of divorce.

By her action, she had inadvertently handed her husband license to cheat, as well as enrolled him as a member of the Cheaters Club. In the next few months (if she hadn't yet joined) she would be a member herself.

At the end of the day, both husband and wife (parents to two wonderful children, five and three years old) had only succeeded in being active participants in the self syndrome. If any member of their family is cheated, it is their children. This time, they cheated on their children.

When we fail to quickly reconcile a hurt in a marital relationship, we open the door for a long journey into the wilderness of separation and divorce. In this kingdom, the devil is the king, and there are too many giants to contend with. Unfortunately, none of the giants will ever lead the couple back to the vineyard of peace. Their primary ambition is to plant hostility through destructive jargon like "irreconcilable differences", "incompatibility", and the like. These words are an apt description of the character of the enemy of the peace of man—the devil, whose objective remains to steal, kill, and destroy. As occasion warrants, spouses should honor each other with reconciliation over little issues in the household.

"Ursula, age twenty-four is about the beginning of the journey to account for the W of your marriage. Isn't it far better to reunite with the man you know than to remarry or be with a new man?" She moped at me.

> Therefore if you are offering your
>
> Gift at the altar and there remember that your brother has
>
> Something against you, leave your gift there in front of the
>
> Altar and Go and be reconciled to your brother, then come
>
> And offer your gift. (What if the brother is your spouse?)
>
> 25: Settle matters quickly with your adversary who
>
> Is taking you to court. Do it while you are still with him on The way, or he may hand you over to the judge, and the judge may hand you over to the officer, and you may be Thrown into prison.
>
> 26: I tell you the truth you may not
>
> Get out until you have paid the last penny. (Matthew 5:24–26)

Christian couples need to get out of the prison of irreconcilable differences and incompatibility through applying the principle of the five-fold ministry of reconciliation, understanding that we who live, no longer live for ourselves, by canceling trespasses as often as they occur, as Christ canceled ours, declaring every hurt an old thing that should be allowed to pass away. Once we could misunderstand as individuals. Now we have got to go under each other to stand as ones welded, bonded, and melted together as one, who should also reconcile as one. And, finally, as God was in Christ reconciling us to Himself, so we should let the Christ in us reconcile us in times of issues and challenges by beholding and creating a new atmosphere of peace out of any adverse situation.

As Christ Loved the Church

> Husbands, love your wives, even as Christ also loved the church, and gave himself for it. (Ephesians 5:25)

As Christ loved the church. This is the standard of God for man in His manual of life, the Bible. If every husband complied with this instruction in the manual, every home would be a haven of peace, love, and godliness. How did Christ love the church?

1. He was sacrificial in His love. Jesus left His position in the Trinity and Glory and took on the form of man in pursuit of the redemption of mankind. He left His Glory heavenly insignia and became a mere man, a mere mortal, with all human limitations. He came to seek and save, sanctify and satisfy us. He came to give abundant life. He came to heal and deliver man from sickness and bondage.
The husband has such enormous responsibility. God expects the man to leave his ego and power and condescend. Every man who desires to keep his power must be weak! Strength is made perfect in weakness. You must seek to make your wife happy. You must seek to satisfy her. You must come down if you want her to revere you. Jesus came down to us. Now, we revere Him. His name is above every name.
2. He gave. Love gives. God so loved the world that He gave His only begotten son. The equation would be incomplete if the only begotten son did not lay down his life. Jesus gave Himself in exchange for our redemption. When Abraham credit for giving his only son Isaac, it should be considered

that he was act old man. The young lad could have shoved him aside and escape f murderous arms. Isaac submitted at the altar of oblation. He yielded completely to be slain according to the will of God.

Dear husband, give. Give your spouse your unconditional love. Give her your time in constant conversation. Give her your energy in domestic affairs. Give her spiritual, material, and emotional support. Give, give, and never stop giving!

3. He loved the church to the end. John 13:1: Having loved his own which we world, he loved them unto the end.

   His love was not short-lived. It could not be short-circuited by any unpleasant circumstance. His love was total, genuine, and irreversible.

   If a man loves his wife to the end, he will neither walk away from the marriage nor aid her to walk away by his misdemeanor. When a wife seeks divorce, it is an indication that he has not loved her to the end. Let your love to and for your wife be unending. Let it be an unbroken circuit. Let it be a circle; a ring of love. Like the love of God, love her with an everlasting love.

4. His love was patient. The imperfection of His disciples did not deter Him. H Judas friend when he led a band of soldiers to arrest Him. He told Peter to net at the right side of the sea of Tiberias after he betrayed and forsook Him gospel. He organized a closed-door meeting with people that abandoned Him into the cruel hands of soldiers. His love was patient. He was tolerant.

How patient are you, husband? How tolerant are you with your wife? Are you easily irritated? Do you bear with her as unto the weaker vessel? Do you have one of your eyes closed in your relationship? It is excellent to have both eyes open when you are looking for a wife, but once you have her, close one of your eyes. Overlook when necessary. The eye that is closed never sees her errors. The one that is open detects and fixes things without stirring the hornet's nest. It cleans the spilt milk, covers the pot, shuts the kitchen door, replaces water containers in the refrigerator, wipes the dusty television, places the remote control on the table, mops the wet floor, flushes the used toilet, and fixes lots of things without making any fuss.

Are your two eyes open? You will certainly find faults in your spouse. Close one and open the other for the purpose of fixing the errors. The charge to love is a direct instruction to the man: husbands, love your wife. Do you seek an everlasting marriage? The key is love. Love your wife as Christ loved the church.

Secret Three. Remember to love your wife as Christ loved the church. How? He was prepared to give his life for the church.

Close one eye to her faults and open the other for reconciliation.

CHAPTER 4

The Two "-Ings" of Marriage

The words *enjoying* and *enduring* bear the suffix *-ing* that marks the title of this chapter.

When Ms. Cindy from Florida told me that she did not think "My marriage to my husband is of God," I told her that I had heard that before, from Atlanta, New York, Sacramento, from coast to coast and across America. She belonged to the set of spouses who absolve themselves of issues and challenges they brought into their marriages by placing the blame on God. When people express such emotions, it is so easy for me to understand that they lack deeper knowledge of marriage.

"Pastor Harry, my marriage is not of God."

"Nope! Please stop there." Then I follow up with the question, "Is the journey from Egypt to Canaan of God?" Their answer usually is "Ye, yee, yeep!"

"Then what happened?" I don't usually wait for an answer. What happened is that God promised to get the people of Israel to the land of promise in four days. But they ended up running around the wilderness for forty years —not because of God's inability to keep His own side of the bargain. Nope! It was because of their disobedience. The children of Israel found it difficult to transit from "enjoying" Egypt to "enduring" the wilderness.

So it is with marriage: the problems and challenges are not God made. Neither are they because God made mistakes. No, God never makes mistakes. Marriage is his second investment in humanity, after creation. To get to Canaan, God's people must drop the defilements of Egypt. For us to enjoy marriage, we must drop the defilement of our past life. Every problem of modern marriage is a result of people ignoring Christ and the principles He taught.

More often, spouses make the same mistakes people of the world make by thinking that they can know the saving name of our Lord Jesus Christ without applying the principles He taught. Teach me the definition of religion. Tell me about self-righteousness. But the truth is that the principles activate the miracle that is in the name of the Lord.

A cell phone is worthless in the hand of the owner until the principle of activation is applied. Check this out: the sheriff and cops will still give you ticket even if you drop the name of President Obama as your classmate at Harvard. But when you remember the image of the president as your classmate in Harvard and apply the tenets of the law of the land as outlined in the constitution of America, your redemption from a ticket is automatic. The truth is that it is not about the president of United States; it is about the constitution of the country.

The Bible is the constitution of the world. Every tenet of the constitutions of countries of the world derives from the Bible: tax for tithe, government, delegation, division of labor—they are too numerous to mention. People obey the laws of their offices, countries, and social clubs, but they will never obey the words of God concerning marriage. You cannot bring your old defiled life as single man or woman to your new (holy matrimony) marriage and expect to enjoy your marriage. It does not work like that. Once we give our lives to Christ, we must give our marriages to Christ, making sure our marriages are also regenerated.

"My marriage is not of God!" That's your opinion, sister. My opinion is from the Bible, and it says that God formed man but made the woman. Let's follow the sequence from the beginning in the King James Version of the Bible. Chapter 2:7: He formed man. After waiting awhile, one could hear God soliloquize in verse 18b, "I will make him a help meet." Yet in verse 19 He continued forming stuff from out of the ground—beast of the field, every fowl of the air, and so on. In verse 20b, we hear Him soliloquize again: "but for Adam there was not found a help meet."

In making a woman, three things are noteworthy from a literary point of view. First God has to put Adam to sleep. Anesthesia makes a patient powerless in the hand of a medical doctor, making it easy to take away what will not help the patient to replace it with what will. After this long wait, the woman was made to take care of his areas of deficiency and weaknesses.

Secondly the words *make* and *made* we see in the King James Version literally present the picture of an architect or creative artist who makes a design unique to a specific purpose or for a particular person.

Thirdly, after God deposited all the good qualities a woman should bring into the home of Adam, He "brought" Eve to Adam. Two key words hold the foundation of heaven, even our faith. They are *peace* and *obedience*. Adam displayed both when he woke up.

The question is "Is my marriage to my husband of God?" The answer is yes, because only God brings husband and wife together, period. They do the marrying, not God. God only provides a book of guidance (the Bible), and if they cherish it, their marriage becomes enjoyable. But if they ignore it, they bring in defilement, which in turn results in having to *endure* it.

The Bible still holds the truth that without defilement, every marriage is honorable. Honorable simply means loving things that God loves. Dishonorable simply means loving things that God hates. The book of Leviticus talks about making common the holy things of God.

God brought a perfectly finished woman to Adam, adorning her with the necessary equipment to complement every area of his deficiencies. The Almighty God never matches two spouses with the same negative character traits; the man may be quick-tempered (like Nadab), but the woman is moderately tempered (like Abigail). The woman may be casual and loquacious (like Job's wife), but the man will be calm, calculated, and spiritual, like Job. One attitude complements or counteracts the other: no negative to negative. And no positive to positive. In fact, no bumper to bumper! Either we have Ahab married to Jezebel, or we have Jezebel married to Ahab.

So married couples who think their marriages are not of God should retrace their steps back to the altar and seek godly counsel from pastors who are successful in marriage. Yes, because they are victims of disobedience. At the altar, they obtained God's blessings but dropped them at the reception table and went for the honeymoon. The knowledge to obtain here is that the wedding is not the marriage.

Marriage starts after the wedding, when rented limousines and tuxedos are returned. Couples who dropped their marriages at the wedding reception and rushed for the honeymoon will return seeing the moon but never tasting the honey. The solution lies in the rededication of the marriage and renewing the vows before a credible minister of the gospel. So wherever couples met before their wedding was where God brought them to meet each other.

Maybe you were studying science at the college library. Perhaps you attended the same high school, college, or university. Maybe you met at the airport or even passed on your way to the airplane restroom. You sat beside each other on the plane, bus, or airport shuttle. That's where God positioned you so He could bring you to each other.

Make no mistake about it—God has the capacity and capability to stop the marriage if it is not of Him. Spouses should not waste time wondering whether their marriage is of God. They should spend time seeking solutions and stop being part of the problem. One wink from the man or woman can restrain an action that will save a nation.

In the secular world, Caesar's wife warned her husband. In the spiritual world, Herod's and Haman's wives warned them. This is what I refer to as *elasticity of God's grace*. A woman's uniqueness is fulfilled when she lives with her husband in a complementary relationship, not in competition.

The Joy in Enjoying

The way to the palace of enjoying marriage is JOY. Couples that observe this acronym never endure marriage; they enjoy it abundantly. Remember: the Bible says the joy of the Lord is our strength.

In marriage, Jesus is first, your spouse is second, and you are third. This is the JOY I am talking about. This is the JOY that leads to enjoyment.

J: Jesus first

O: Others second Y: You third

JOY makes you empty yourself for your partner.

JOY destroys the venom and asp of self.

JOY chases out the spirit of greed and avarice.

JOY encourages you to celebrate your spouse.

JOY points you to the bigger picture of marriage.

JOY kills pride and enshrines humility.

JOY oozes out the fruit of the Spirit in you.

JOY challenges your partner to outdo you in the game, thereby making your home a haven of peace, love, and enjoyment.

Your marriage is in your hand to enjoy or to endure. To the man, your wife is your first child before your first child. Truly, when God formed Adam from the dust of the earth and breathed into him the breath of life, He conceived Eve in his inside. Adam was pregnant with Eve! God simply performed a caesarian and brought the mature baby out of him. The same with the woman: your husband is the first son before your first son. Eve had no son initially. Adam was the only son available in the garden for her to nurture. She catered for him. She cuddled him like a baby. Adam indeed was a mature baby. How you handle each other will determine whether you will enjoy or endure your marriage. The good news is that you can move from enduring to enjoying with very little guidance from the Bible. May the Lord transform your marriage to permanent enjoyment!

Values That Make a Positive -Ing

The -ings of marriage carry both negative and positive characters: enduring and enjoying. Marriage is meant to be enjoyed, not endured. When the right cards are brought to the table, the -ing becomes positive.

There are certain values the psalmist listed in Psalm 15 as behavioral pattern for those who will ascend the holy place of the Lord. Heaven is a holy place. So is the marital home. God dwells in a home that honors Him above everything in the world. Check yourself in this mirror.

Integrity. Do you have integrity? Do you keep your promises? Stand by your words. Let not your mouth be like a dual carriage. Your spouse should know you for your impeccable integrity.

Truth. Are you truthful? Truth must be the guiding principle of your life as a spouse. Let your words express truth always. Let your partner take your words as the truth, nothing but the truth. Let your yea be yea and your nay be nay.

Humility. You cannot be as proud as a peacock and attempt to attract the positive -ing: enjoying. Let this virtue be seen in your relationship. Let this humble disposition with your spouse be obvious.

Respect. Do you have respect for your spouse? Are you a bully? Do you treat her with disdain? Is it your habit to despise him because you pay the bills?

Kindness. How kind are your words and actions to your partner and children? Do you have healthy relationships with them? God is watching!

Honesty. Honesty is a key value. Without it, you will renege on your commitments. Are you honest in your commitments with your partner? Be honest in all you do.

Accountability. You must be accountable to be able to inculcate this value in your spouse. You must show plain accountability in your office, business, and services to God and man. Live it, teach it. That's the way!

Justice. This value will keep you far away from selfish conclusions. It will help you esteem fairness and equity. You will be pomp, plain and objective in all ways and issues. Let this value be a front burner in your life.

Obedience. How obedient are you to the word of God? Do you uphold the principles and patterns of God? Demonstrate implicit obedience to God! Let your obedience be complete. Then God will avenge every disobedience.

Self-control. Do you have self-control? Do you have control over your emotions, behavior, and appetite?

Sexual purity. Are you immoral? The answer is yes or no. There is no other way around it. Do you flirt around? Do you jest or idle away with the opposite sex in immoral talk? Be wise. Set a high moral value and keep it!

Secret Four. Your marriage is of God. God does not allow what He did not approve to come to manifestation. Your husband is your first son before your first biological son. Conversely, your wife is your first daughter before your first biological child. Treat, nurse, and nurture yourselves like you would your first son and first daughter, and you set a good platform for everlasting enjoyment of your marriage.

CHAPTER 5

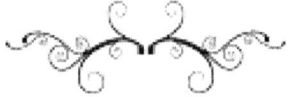

Embracing the F-Word

When love and vision have suffered shipwreck in marriage, the first words to avoid are "It's over." Rather, spouses should clear their minds and hearts and be prepared to apply the F-word: forgiveness.

Forgiveness becomes the linking wire that should rekindle love. Yet forgiveness is one virtue that is difficult to obtain in marital relationships.

> If thou shall confess with thy mouth, the Lord Jesus, and shall believe in thine heart that God hath raised him from the dead, thou shall be saved. (Romans 10:9)

This is the core of our faith as Christians. There is an everlasting peace and joy for people who are not only saved as a result of confessing the Lord Jesus (as their Lord and personal Savior) but have also taken time to confess Him as the Lord (and personal Savior) of their marriages. The expectation from such spouses is that when division creeps into the marriage, whoever is at fault should confess to the other *that the marriage may be saved.*

Living Word Ministries is a total gospel ministry that has impacted the lives of the Nigerian community in diverse forms: Mission Hospital, Bible-based practical application training center, dynamic church plants, and now a university. As the director of the Christian Men's Forum of this great ministry, I once organized a workshop for men; the topic was "Husbanding a Quick-Tempered Wife." Some of the conclusions we arrived at in that workshop, using Job's wife as a reference point, are as follow:

a) Quick-tempered wives are the best friends of the enemy of marriages (Sat the devil). In 1 Peter 5:8, we see a very strong counsel to spouses, which Jo wife did not observe or obey. Peter's wise counsel is:
"Be wise, be vigilant, because your adversary the devil walks about like a roaring lion, seeking whom he may devour."
Verse 9 started with a strict and strong command: "Resist him."
In working on self-control and anger management, spouses with this kind of vice should wear the garment of forgiveness 24-7.

b) Letting the adversary into their homes is a choice made by those who are insensitive to the ways of the adversary: subtle, working on the imagination couples to misread, misjudge, and misinterpret each other's intentions a actions, attaching negative conclusions and connotations to simple acts affection.

c) Job's wife is a case of insensitivity. She missed it when she fell into the t of a wicked enemy who proudly confessed to God in Job 1:7 that was preoccupation is "going to and fro on the earth, and from walking back a forth on it."

Job's wife was neither wise nor vigilant. She not only became a victim of "roaring lion who was seeking whom to devour," she became the "whom" used to devour her marriage. This situation is still rampant among modern spouses. In order to avoid problems, spouses should be careful not to be the ones to attract the devourer.

At any point that spouses allow the unholy visitation of the adversary into their homes, very small issues develop from misunderstanding to quarrels. If not tackled immediately, it progresses from grudge to bitterness. If it is left to drag on, pride provides a platform for the unforgiving spirit to step in.

Unforgiveness in marriage is a cancer that has no immediate or prolonged remedy. The elimination or duration of the cure is in the hand of spouses. A quick-tempered wife who has no self-control can run her temper anywhere, anytime, with little provocation. Her husband must decorate himself with the garment of forgiveness if he wants to honor God with his marriage.

Bob and Therese are a wonderful couple in Los Angeles. They had formed a habit at the early days of their marriage to take a shower together every morning. That habit later became a point of contact for reconciliation after any marital misunderstanding. It does not matter the level of hostility all through their day or night, one person must announce, "Shower t-t-i-m-e-e!" in the morning. That is the miracle wand that produced tacit and unspoken reconciliation daily.

I ask you a question: "What habit are you bringing to the matrimonial table that will act as a platform for reconciliation when your marriage is challenged by issues of the day?"

Charles, in San Jose, California, does not allow a breakdown in the relationship between him and Comfort to linger on for too long. After a while, he moves over to grab her on the backside while she is preparing dinner for the family. Comfort would usually turn her head back to him with a small grin. Having done that, Comfort follows up in the night by wearing his favorite night perfume to bed. And this time, "I am the one that grabs his backside." And that's it. I wouldn't think out some stuff for you and your spouse. The time to stop living as roommates and strange bedfellows is now. Drown division and get down with the vision of your marriage. Enthrone forgiveness as a way of life.

John Bello, my editor in Nigeria, and his amiable wife, Sarah, have their melting points. It doesn't matter the weight of acrimony, and it doesn't matter who stirred the hornet's nest; John would usually buy Sarah a gift on his way from the office. Rather than get upset with her, he would put the gift in her hand upon opening the door to the bedroom. Sarah has her joker too. She usually said, "Shall we pray?" at bedtime. That always ended any rancor. It is always easy to talk things through after either card (John's gift or Sarah's "Shall we pray?") is placed on the table.

Different couples, different strokes. Anna simply throws her leg across Dave's as he passes her by. And that's it. Dave "retaliates" with a grin and a new sort of eyeing. There is actually no big deal about reconciliation and forgiveness if we extricate pride from our relationship with our spouse.

Couples should do something to rekindle relationships, lighting a fresh fire. And whatever is done with a good heart should be reciprocated by the other. However, when all applications fail to restore a relationship, then a review of this scenario is recommended.

A good Christian spouse has unguardedly allowed a very serious misunderstanding to suddenly creep into a household discussion. A little indiscretion turns into a hot exchange of words of anger and hostility. This situation developed until husband-and-wife face opposite directions at bedtime.

Picture this: in the morning, the woman wakes up, taps the husband, and says to him, "I am going to make breakfast. I want to make sure you don't leave the house without refreshing yourself with the breakfast I'm going to make for you."

And the husband? He wakes up after some minutes, walks straight to the kitchen, and says, "My love, when you want to get ready for your job, call me so I can iron your clothes/uniform, okay?"

What a way to reconnect, from hostility to hospitality. When a spouse takes a humbling and sacrificial step to work on restoring hospitality in a home and achieves a tasteful result, neither spouse will be in a hurry to rock the boat in the future. Wherever hospitality replaces hostility, the end result is an uncommon miracle. Spouses should be in a hurry to restore order and friendship in the home. That is the only way forgiveness will become a way of life. Our Lord Jesus is interested in restorative correction and not damnable condemnation; hear him:

> Simon, Simon, indeed, Satan has asked for you that he may sift you, as wheat. But I have prayed for you, that your faith should not fail;
>
> and when you have returned to Me, strengthen your brethren. (Luke 22:31–32)

In other words, our Lord forgave Peter (prayerfully) before he informed him. Simple admonition, no condemnation, but with a view to restore. And with an instruction to also restore others that the vision will move on to the shame of the enemy Satan, the devil. Sell your pride and save your love and family.

There is a higher dimension of forgiveness exemplified by Jesus here: *"But I have prayed for you, that your faith should not fail."* Peter had not denied Him at this point. He had not cut off the ear of the high priest's servant; neither had he forsaken him together with other disciples. What Jesus did was advance forgiveness. He forgave Peter before he even denied him. He did not even wait for Peter to ask for forgiveness. He had his eraser handy before Peter wrote with his pencil.

How wonderful our homes would be if we learned to forgive simultaneously as offenses are committed. Our homes would be havens of peace, love, and joy if we enlarged our capacity to forgive in advance. We would not be edgy, and our spouses would not be repulsive in our sight. We would tolerate each other in the spirit of love.

When the mind and heart are centered on a vision, forgiveness becomes a matter of course. The vision of the New Testament was first revealed to Peter by "my father in heaven"—not through flesh and blood: Matthew 16:18.

But, unfortunately, from the book of Matthew, when the church was revealed to the book of Acts when the church was born, Peter made too many mistakes. Our Lord Jesus knew more than enough not to let unforgiveness distract the journey of the birth of the church through Peter. Peter cut off the ear of a servant of the high priest; the Lord forgave and repaired what he spoilt. Peter denied the Lord three times. The Lord forgave him again. Our ever-wise Jesus would not let the devil short-circuit the vision of the New Testament church through a series of attacks on Peter, the man upon whose confession the church would be birthed.

So Peter was forgiven several mistakes, the greatest of which is going back to fishing after he had been ordained fisher of men. Can you please stop here and imagine how the Lord restored Peter through an extraordinary and creative act of forgiveness? Everything the Lord came for was being rocked through Peter's act of insubordination. He not only deceived himself, he sabotaged the vision by leading the other eleven astray with three simple words that had the power and authority of a leader: "I go afishing."

Don't Give Up on Your Spouse!

God will not give up on us. He is ever faithful to keep us even in our down times. When Adam and Eve disobeyed God in the Garden of Eden, God clothed them from their nakedness. He could have destroyed them immediately and created another man and woman. No, not God. He is merciful and loving. He is a God of many chances.

UNENDING MARITAL BLESSINGS

"It's over!" This is the language of the unsaved couple. Clothe your wife instead of walking out on her for another woman. Clothe your husband rather than move out to hook up with another. God clothed the first parents instead of sacking them for their misdemeanor.

In Luke chapter 5, Peter fished all night and caught nothing. Just as he began washing the empty net to go home, Jesus came up to save his face from ridicule and frustration. He let down the net rather than wash it and quit. Don't wash your marital net yet. Jesus stands before you, urging you to let down your net. Let down your net! There is a lot of fun to still catch in the ocean of love. There is a lot of joy and satisfaction to catch.

Let me give you a quick synopsis of the disciples Jesus raised. He was surrounded by people of different shades of character. Jesus managed them all. They were all carnal and religious in their relationship with Jesus. Judas Iscariot betrayed his master with a kiss. Earlier on, John and James secretly went with their mother to secure positions in the kingdom. The other disciples were filled with indignation when they discovered what John and James allowed their mother to do. Jesus was not.

Hold on—I am not done yet! All the disciples argued among themselves over who should be the greatest. When Jesus was denied entry through Samaria, the two disciples were poised to call fire down from heaven to destroy the people. Peter denied him not once but three times. He had earlier brought out sword to cut off somebody's ear.

At the garden of Gethsemane, they could not tarry in prayer with Jesus. They were too weak to bear the burden of ministry. When their master was arrested, they all fled and forsook him. Thomas doubted his resurrection. In fact, Peter led all of them back to fishing, forsaking the gospel entrusted in their hands.

This is the crop of disciples that surrounded Jesus. At resurrection, they were the same set of people Jesus was ready to meet in Galilee. He met them in Galilee, their point of weakness. He met them at the point of their inabilities. He was ready to change them. He was ready to break their circuits and give them wings to fly. He knew they would not be able to do His will without His help.

> Then said Jesus unto them, Be not afraid: go tell my brethren that they go into Galilee, and there shall they see me. (Matthew 28:10)

There are two quick lessons to learn from this verse of the Bible.

1. Go tell my brethren. Jesus called them brethren, the same people that forsoo the time he needed moral support. The same people that could not carry His with Him. He did not judge them by their repeated misdemeanors. He castigate Peter for denying Him.
2. Go tell my brethren that they go into Galilee. Jesus met them at Galilee. He initiative to meet them. He took the first step toward gathering them. He himself to them in Galilee and commissioned them to preach the gospel to the world.

How could He trust such people to be faithful in His absence when they were unfaithful in His presence? How could He trust a man who denied Him three times? How could He still reckon with people that forsook Him in His trial moment?

Oh, God is gracious! He is merciful. We are the extension of His grace and mercy. The manner of offense doesn't matter; let us remain friends and not fiends. Our common foe is the devil. Like Jesus called people who neglected Him brethren, call your wife by her pet name always, in good and bad times. Regard your husband at all times.

Let us put into action the nature of God in us. We are partakers of

His divine nature. Man gets, gets, and forgets. God gives, gives, and forgives. Let us give: give peace, give joy, give love, love patience, give kindness, give… Let us forgive always.

Rather than go gaga with words of anger; rather than express authority and power over the disobedient; rather than confront their misdemeanor, our Lord, step by gradual step, brought the disciples back to the vision, to the point where he invited them to enjoy breakfast. In other words, you can still have what you are struggling for without disobeying the word or rocking the vision. "Children!" referring to mature grownups: "Children! Have you any meat?" (John 21:5) Peter and the disciples were restored. Then Peter received the second and last call: "Follow me." That's the call that gave birth to the vision of the church in Acts 2. The act of forgiveness therefore became the bedrock of the birth of the New Testament church. Jesus trashed the offense and redeemed the offender (Peter) to continue with the vision. Spouses should learn to trash each other's offenses and redeem their love for each other.

How can we talk about Stephen, who forgave those who were raining stones on him when he saw the son of man watching? This is a big lesson to spouses. Look up as you make that quarrelsome decision and see the Prince of Peace watching you and your spouse. Then make a determination to observe peace through forgiveness.

Strengthen yourselves with good words, and move on. The goal and vision is greater than the hurt. There is something that passeth all understanding. It is peace. Don't only seek for it, fight for peace. "Onye ekwele uzo gaa, in tongues." (Let nobody break the rank of peace.)

Secret Five. Put on the garment of forgiveness 24-7 and make up your mind to forgive your spouse in advance of any kind of hurt. Simple acts, very simply acts, can restore, refire, and reignite freshness in the relationship. Remember.

DR. HARRY TOBECHI NZE

The enemy will always desire to sift your marriage. Both of you must make up your minds not to be sifted.

CHAPTER 6

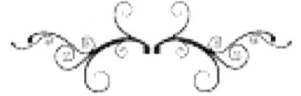

Embracing the F-Word, Reloaded

Besides all this, you can ask God for grace to apply biblical principles. Remember that my definition of the Bible is "The ancient book that is modern by application."

In Acts chapter 6, the number one vision on the disciples' to-do list was to move the word of God forward. But with the multiplication of disciples came "di-vision." With division came murmuring.

In the United States, irrespective of the preparations, the arrival of a new baby brings multiplication of stuff. This is because a new baby truncates the status quo. There is stuff to buy. There are rearrangements to make in the house. Job schedules are affected. If it is an average household, a third party (a nanny) moves in. What about extra money for baby food, a car seat, toys, and stuff? If not well handled by spouses, this bundle of joy will produce bundle of divisions, and divisions, by nature, lead to murmuring. Murmuring produces quarrels and bickering; those are the grandmothers of unforgiveness.

The scenario is different in Africa. When a new baby arrives in Africa, the couple steps aside while family members struggle to outdo each other, striving to provide a diversity of foodstuff: all kinds of baby food and food for mother.

If you are a reader of this book in the United States, please know that when there is an increase in the household as a result of a new baby, it is a big challenge. Settle it in your heart to do what the disciples did.

    a) Call a spousal conference and redefine duties to ease tension in house.
When spouses observe genuine desire to ease the burden of multiplication, the vision of the marriage is oiled, while division is starved of oil. Soon its engine is ready for the trash. Forgiveness is the core engine of a good marriage.

    b) Do what Stephen did: call the author of marriage not to "lay this sin unforgiveness) upon their (your spouse's) charge," and thereafter move on. What a heart! Under very extreme pain, Stephen was able to forgive those who subjected him to the pain of stones. He did not do it by flesh but by being full of the Holy Ghost and also as he "looked up Steadfast into heaven and saw the glory of God and Jesus Standing at the rig hand of God. (Acts 6:55)
Can I ask you a personal question? When was the last time you took a challenge in the household to the author of marriage, God Almighty?
It's a personal question; therefore, record your personal answer for your use.
Can I ask you another personal question? When was the last time you did this:

    c) In a spousal conference, write down the stuff that is causing division between you and your spouse; read them out to one another. Taking notes of what each person wrote, apologizing to each other, and exchange your paper or note. Let each person tear the one in his or her hand.
See how the Lord handled forgiveness:

> But Jesus stooped down and with his finger
>
> Wrote on the ground as though He heard them not. (John 8:6)

Later, in verse 11, He cleansed the woman, forgave her sins, and pointed her to her future. Biblical forgiveness blots the offense as if it did not happen and must always open a new front in future relationship. Our Lord cleansed her past and pointed her to her future. What about you? In your tenth year of marriage, you still remind your spouse of stuff you settled five years ago. Too bad!

Spouses should learn from our Lord Jesus Christ, who under extreme provocation by his beloved Peter, referred to him and his cohorts as "children" who were obsessed with a fish breakfast delicacy Africans refer to as "Fish Pepper Soup."

> "Children!," he called them, "have you any meat?" (John 21:5)
>
> Jesus said unto them "Come and dine." Jesus then cometh, and
>
> Taketh bread, and giveth them and fish likewise. (John.21:12–13)

That was a very simple act of forgiveness spouses should emulate—no negative words, no frowning, no mention of a previous act, no bad mouthing about leading the other disciples astray. Jesus focused on Peter and the vision of the church, which he "confessed" in Mathew 16:18 (the past) and the birth that was coming in Acts 2:14 (the future). The uniqueness of biblical forgiveness is that it must trash the past and point to the future. Between the book of Mathew, when the confession of the church was made, and Acts, when the church was birthed, our Lord Jesus forgave Peter several times.

Watch this: only those who came to marriage with child and spousal support in mind keep a diary of offenses; Christians should not. Yes, because there is already a "woe" to whomsoever offenses shall come through, because whether we like it or not:

> It is impossible that offenses will come but woe unto him Through whom they come. (Luke 17:1 KJV)

> Jesus said to his disciples: "Things that make people sin are Bound to happen, but how terrible for the one who makes it happen." (GNB)

Now read my translation: "Unforgiveness is a sin that produces generational curses. I will not let me be the one to bring it to dwell in my household. I will always seek simple acts to forgive."

> This is because whatever sin I forgive is forgiven. Whatever sin I did not forgive is retained by me and recycled to my next generation. (John 20:23)

This is how the word *wickedness* became generationally generic in a family. May the Lord deliver His own in Jesus's name. Amen!

Spouses, note this: unforgiveness produces curses and bad words; it rocks the peace, produces pride, competition, presumptions and assumptions, imagination, grudges—name them; you know them. Whenever you find yourself under extreme provocation by your spouse, remember that it was simple act of forgiveness and patience that gave birth to the church. May the Lord open your eyes to see how unforgiveness has stunted the growth of your household and family. You could have done better but for the scourge called *unforgiveness*.

From now on, when your spouse offends you, simply look at him or her as a child; put your head on his or her shoulder and move on, for the vision of caring for a family on behalf of the Almighty

UNENDING MARITAL BLESSINGS

God is bigger than little hurts here and there.

Joe Littleton was supposed to travel to New Jersey for a business conference. So he asked his wife, Kathy, to wake him up by seven thirty in the morning so he could ready himself to catch the nine o'clock flight. But thirty minutes after that, Joe and Kathy had a little misunderstanding, and they began to have an attitude for each other. Suddenly they stopped talking to each other. Kathy left to her job by seven, with a note beside Joe on the bed: "Wake up by seven thirty and prepare for your New Jersey flight by nine." Joe woke at nine fifteen. His wife had gone to her job, and the note was right there on his side of the bed. He quickly called the airline. The flight was gone. He was rescheduled for the second flight. He arrived in New Jersey as the conference was rounding up. He lost his job.

The Littletons did not have a tradition of ignoring little hurts and moving on. Do one thing: embrace forgiveness *now* and move your love life and family on.

Secret Six. When your spouse hurts you, simply look at him or her as a child. Jesus did! Then put your head on his or her shoulder and move on. You can move on to your spouse's favorite eatery. Bring home a bunch of his or her "usual." Set it up and invite him or her over. Jesus did!

CHAPTER 7

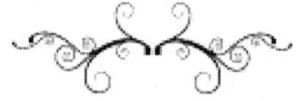

Better Reuniting Than Remarrying

The Covenant Sisters Fellowship that Angela began in Los Angeles in 2003 emerged into one of the most successful women's ministries subsequent to the Unique Women Fellowship International of Living Word Ministries.

She came with the impartation of Mrs. Chinyere-Emma Okorie, a gifted and anointed prophetic conference speaker, who allowed Angela to represent her at key speaking engagements in Africa.

Equipped with a trickling-down experience as a member of the Central Ministry's board of the Unique Women's Fellowship, Angela gave a solid base to the Unique Women's Fellowship Chapter at the Word Fellowship Christian Center. We praise God. Word Fellowship Christian Center in time became the regional headquarters that housed three other churches. By the Lord's special favor, I was the pastor of WFCC region. We are especially thankful to God that WFCC gained the reputation of becoming the best organized women's ministry of the more than thirty churches planted by the Living Word Ministries. We are also especially thankful and blessed that many mature and gifted leadership team members of the central ministry (both men and women) were a vital part of WFCC region.

In addition to all these, I was appointed the chairman of the church Plant Committee, with a mandate to plant and/or revive six churches in different cities of Nigeria. Almost at that same period, Angela was also mandated by the central ministry to plant the Unique Women's Fellowship in such African cities as Portharcourt, Owerri, and Umuahia. Grace is an unmerited favor. Mercy is unmerited pardon. The Lord lavished both on us and helped us achieve all the mandated challenges to His glory.

This incredible experience, coupled with the transparent love of the Lord, provided the catalyst for the explosive growth of Covenant Sisters Fellowship in Los Angeles and later in Phoenix, Arizona.

Growing up in the Christian faith, we were trained, groomed, and equipped for service at the Living Word Training Center, an international school of Practical Bible Application with centers in the USA and Africa.

Meeting of the Covenant Sisters Fellowship

The weekend of the next meeting of the Covenant Sisters, Angela was scheduled to travel to Minnesota, and I was to hold brief for her.

Please be aware that the Covenant Sisters Fellowship was made up of successful career women in nursing and business with a diversity of interests and disciplines: money, second degrees, personable husbands, and grown children. Some of them were determined to grow as good Christians. Fortunately, unlike the Samaritan woman, none of them had remarried, not even once.

It became obvious that I would need the comfort of the Holy Spirit to get across to these wonderful women. Like always, He revealed to me the topic – Better Reunite Than Remarry.

Come that Sunday evening, as I stood before them, I discovered that as sure as gunshot these were women who were so content that they could look Elisha straight at the face and say:

> No, I am perfectly content. (2 Kings 4:12 LB)
>
> No, my family takes good care of me. (NIV)
>
> I have all I need here among my own people. (GN)
>
> "I dwell among my own people, they are sufficient." (AMP)

My translation? "Honey, I work for my money. I don't need stuff from nobody. Baby, am cooooool!" MiTLN

However, like the Shunamite woman, some of them lacked one thing or the other. The majority were single parents and unmarried singles. Fortunately, unlike the Samaritan woman who married five times, none of them had remarried. How apt can the Holy Spirit be in appointing an appropriate topic to share with these wonderful women who surreptitiously became victims of cultural environment? A quick prayer, and we were ready to go.

The Wilderness of Divorce

I have come here this evening not only to seek to preserve marriages but to save lives.

Let me thank you for the opportunity to be here this evening. Let's start this way. How many people in this hall tonight are thinking of separating from their husbands, thinking of divorce, or are already divorced. More than threequarters of the hands went up. Then I asked another question: "How many of the sisters here tonight are believers married to unbelievers?" Almost the same number.

I have come as a servant of God with one short message: better to reunite than remarry. I have also come this night with one short advice: stop that move, and make that move.

There are four sets of people in this hall tonight.

a) Those who are thinking of separating from their husbands
b) Those who are already separated and have custody of the children
c) Those who are legally divorced and hoping for a "second mission a journey"
d) And the single sisters who are progressive in age who desire to be sett in their own homes

I would like to talk about each of the four situations, one after the other, believing God that He will help me draw from my wealth of experience as a pastor and biblical counselor – and teach you all from what he taught me over the years.

Hear me, folks. We have lived the sweetest periods of our lives as human beings: *nine months*! That was when God was completely and absolutely in charge, and we did not have an opinion, idea, or suggestion of how He kept us alive under the roof of our mother's womb. Likewise, I say to you that the sweetest part of our lives as married spouses is when we are still where we have identity: under our husband's roof. If we submit to him as a helpless child in the mother's womb, God Almighty, who looked at those weaknesses in him that trip us, will certainly come behind you to fix the issues that are about to lead you or have led you to the wilderness of divorce. The wilderness of divorce is fraught with disobedience to God's instructions. And three things happen when we hit the wilderness of disobedience:

a) You live in further disobedience.
b) You roam the wilderness for years, with no God to direct, guide, protect you all the way. And under-aged and overgrown children seek water (insult) your garden.
c) You take away the children from God's purpose for their

> lives.
> And many (how many?) of the children of Israel shall He (the Child in your custody who is denied joint parental care) turn to the Lord their God. (Luke 1:16–17)
> And he shall go … to turn the hearts of the fathers to the children, and the disobedient to the wisdom of the just; to make ready a people prepared for the Lord.
> (Luke 1: 17b)

This is God's purpose and assignment for your child through his father. And for this reason, despite his shortcomings and your personal diagnoses and expectations for your most ideal husband, God Almighty sent you to husband this one man for Him.

Folks! Many things happen in the wilderness of divorce. So the earlier we understand that your marriage is a divine assignment from God and that husbanding your spouse is a ministry unto the Lord, the better. Leadership, eldership, pastorship are ministries from the Lord. The Lord simply posts members for us to shepherd on His behalf. So it is in marriage—every spouse is on divine assignment from the Lord. We have to work out how to fulfill the ministry to please Him. So it is with your spouse. Though the Lord posted him to you, you have to work out how to husband him, by being by his side.

Behind or by the Side

As a growing young man, I heard the adage, "Behind any successful man is a woman." But as I began to study the Bible, I discovered that a wife can only influence her husband to the negative or positive not by being *behind* him but by being *by his side*. The ear into which she will speak is after all by his side and not behind. Whether on the right or left side, his ear is closer to her when she is walking by his side than behind.

Bekky and Leo White (Separation attempt)

When Ms. Bekky White of West Covina, California, called to inform me that she was about to separate from the husband, she'd already made hotel reservation for herself and her children. A top professional, she can afford it. Matter of fact, she had been catering for the family. All she wanted was appreciation from her husband. Instead of gratitude, all she got was verbal abuse, curses, and humiliation every day.

It was easy to calm her down by referencing many sisters who hit the wilderness of divorce, having passed through worse situations. Today, I get their calls asking how they can be reconciled to their exes, even if they have to be quarrelling every day. "The wilderness of divorce" is a prescription no servant of God can make for any daughter of Zion.

I opened her eyes to the truth that an unbelieving husband will pretend to be attacking his wife. But he is actually attacking her God. However, wives should know that they are Christians. The burden of the proof of their Christianity does not lie on their husband. It lies on them who are Christians. This is the situation God foreknew when he cautioned believers: "Be ye not unequally yoked *together* with unbelievers. (2 Corinthians 6:14–18)

Any wonder then that before the apostolic church, father Abraham made Eleazer swear an oath to get a wife for Isaac from Isaac's maternal home. Today the church of Jesus Christ is our paternal and maternal home.

Dave and Lillian

In 2004, I prayed with Brother Dave, a wonderful brother in Upland California. Brother Dave is glued to his wife and attached to their children. Every Sunday he comes to church with three children perched on his body, one on the right, the other in his left hand, yet another on his back, holding onto his neck. He wouldn't let his wife, who walks besides him, do any manual labor. That's how much he loved his wife and family. And I always referenced him in the Men's' Fellowship. With a car and an office, a loaded and valuable credit card, he showered love on his wife, Lillian.

However, on bad advice and association, his wife went to court, unjustifiably seeking divorce. My friend Dave sent me to court to plead with her to withdraw the proceedings. She was adamant. So we began to pray for his children. However, after three years of praying, a miraculous verdict was given: Dave was given custody of the three children in a city where their mother resides. She lost out. Awesome God! I can hear you gasp. One year after, Lillian desperately sought for reconciliation. But my friend was not ready.

Believing and Unbelieving Spouses

Our all-knowing God also made provision for how His daughters can remedy the situation, once in it. But they must first understand that the duty of an unbelieving husband is to do the work of his father, the devil. Conversely, the job of a believing wife is to do the work of her father, God Almighty. While the husband tries to dethrone and belittle her God, she must meekly apply biblical principle to counterattack. You must not try to match him word for word or attitude for attitude. If you do, you help him not only degrade your God but mock your Christianity. Please do not blame him. There are things he should know as a husband that he does not know: Stuff like this:

"You husbands must be careful of your wives, being Thoughtful of their needs and honoring them as the weaker sex. Remember that you and your wife are Partners (how many spouses know this?) in receiving God's blessings and if you don't treat her as you should, your prayers will not get ready answers (how many husbands

UNENDING MARITAL BLESSINGS

know this?). And now this word to all of you. You should be like one big happy family, full of sympathy toward each other, loving one another with tender hearts and humble minds. Don't repay evil for evil. Don't snap at those who say unkind things about you. Instead pray for God's help for them, for we are to be kind to others. And God will bless us for it. You want a happy good life, keep control of your tongue guard your lips from telling lies. Turn away from evil and do good. Try to live in peace even if you must run after it to catch and hold it.

> For the Lord is watching his children, listening to their prayers, but the Lord's face is hard against those Who do evil. (1 Peter 3:7-12 LB)

Beloved sisters, is your marriage perishing or about to perish because your husband lacks this knowledge and therefore does not know his responsibility as outlined in this scripture? He deserves sympathy and understanding rather than tongue-lashing. You can take charge of the situation, stop that move, and make a new move toward reconciliation.

> Wives, fit in with your husband's plan; for then if they refuse to listen When you talk to them about the Lord, they will Be won by your respectful, pure behavior. Your godly lives will speak to them better than any words. Don't be concerned about the onward beauty that depends on jewelry or beautiful clothes, or hair arrangements. Be beautiful inside In your hearts with the lasting charm of a gentle and Quiet spirit which is so precious to God. That kind of deep beauty was seen in the saintly women of old, Who trusted God and fitted in with their husbands' plans. Sarah, for instance, obeyed her husband, Abraham, honoring him as head of the house. And If you do the same, you

will be following in her steps like good daughters and doing what is right; then you will not fear offending your husband. (1 Peter 3:1–4)

Now, is it not obvious that your husband does not know the tenets of the above scripture? Get to know this: no human being will ever operate above the revelation or ordinary knowledge of the word of God that he or she knows or possesses.

My advice is simple—very simple: stop that separation move, and make that by-his-side move. Now here is the deal.

Power of Influence

In Genesis 2:7, Eve did something you should do. Be aware that men are too touchy about the authority, power, and dominion God gave them over the family. Eve ignored the three and got Adam through *influence*.

And the first principle in making influence effective is positioning. Eve positioned herself *by the side* of her husband.

Whatever the reason you want to abandon your husband and your children, do one thing tonight. Change your position, and lie by his side. If Eve had stayed by the side of her husband and influenced him to the negative, you can stay by the side of your husband and influence him to the positive. Positively or negatively, you cannot influence your spouse from a distance or from behind. Matter of fact, there are three ways to influence your husband, either by lying by his side and getting his audience or loving his mother (your mother-in-law) or both.

Remember what we said earlier: your husband is your first child before your first child. If your first child deviates from family norms, you can't separate from him or her. You will reverently sit him or her down and do some counseling. Do so tonight. Many men like to be treated as kindly as their moms treated them when they were growing. A woman who approaches his stubbornness with the approach of a mother is respected and listened to as a mother.

Remember that your spouse is first your husband and secondarily your brother. The only difference is that you cannot go to bed with your brother. No family feud or misunderstanding will separate a brother and a sister. They will usually sort it out; they abhor separation and continue to dwell under one roof.

Separation can only separate. It will never join. Nearness joins and rejoins.

Tolerance and patience are the keys, and you can apply them this night. Tonight, sit him down and remind him how you started and how you arrived at the issue that pains both of you. In John chapter 6, our Lord Jesus Christ commanded the disciples to "make the people sit down," and the multitude sat down before he began to feed them. There is something about sitting down. Whether in an interview, office, church, business, or other situation, sitting down draws the spirit of dialogue, patience, tolerance, and peace.

I am going to pray that the Lord will replay the video of your courtship in his mind tonight. There certainly will be a change tomorrow morning.

When Ms. Bekky heard all this, she called the hotel and canceled their reservation. Today the family is knitted and woven together like wool into a sweater; they travel to Las Vegas for vacations every now and then.

Stop that move and make that move. Stay by the side of your spouse, and learn how to use the power of influence to the positive. God left that instrument for the women. Wives of presidents use it to change the course of nations. Wives of commanders in chief use it to change the course of wars. Use influence tonight to deliver your children and family. Marriage is a sacred partnership. No partner should abandon the ship in times of trouble.

There is so much to gain if we persevere and sail the boat to safety. For without God, the lion in the wilderness will devour the divorced and separated. God forbid. Amen.

The Second Cut Is the Deepest

There are some of you who are already separated and divorced. Listen to me: if you and your spouse are still not married to someone new, my advice is *make the move* for reunification. I tell you what: 85 percent of the faults and weaknesses of your first husband are already known to you. What caused your divorce and separation was only 15 percent because you allowed it to. You did not have the knowledge that first and foremost all his weaknesses and faults are what God sent you to perfect in him. Secondly, you did not know that marriage is like a development plan in which each spouse trains the other to live within the ambitions of their initial expectations of their spouses as spinsters and bachelors. When you leave your first love, you leave with one hundred bundles of problems to be experienced in your second marriage, if ever. Yes, if ever, because there are many young unmarried who would rather marry unmarried singles than marry ex-this and ex-that.

The secular music says the "first cut is the deepest," but the Bible and our Lord Jesus came for the second cut. Renewal of mind, reformation, regeneration, rejuvenation, reconciliation, and reunification all are products of a second cut. Their results are usually better than the first. Salvation is a second cut. It takes us from the first cut (old self) to the second (born again). You can experience a second cut by making the reconciliation move. Everybody who had a second cut in the Bible had a better reunification and a better and sweeter future.

David's Return to Jerusalem

The people requested that the king should be returned to his first love and home in Jerusalem. Don't be surprised that your ex is waiting for you to make that move. Like the father of the wise (unjustifiably referred to as prodigal) son, your ex is waiting to embrace you again, but *you must make that move*. What a new life that son enjoyed right from when his hand touched the gate of his father's house. What about Joseph? His second cut and return to reformation started with the shaving of his hair. Can you shave your hair and return to amend the things and give him an opportunity to celebrate you once again?

With God, all things are possible. It was only after Elisha patiently joined Elijah to cross the Jordan that He asked for a hard thing. Sometimes marriage can be a hard thing. But with prayers we can receive God's Nevertheless. God's Nevertheless says, "In spite of the fact that your best is not enough; irrespective of your unworthy efforts; not minding your imperfections and ignoring your days of ignorance and attendant mistakes or sins, I am going to give you a second chance and let you have back the mantle." Folks, God is ready. What about you? All you need do is stop that move and make that move. I will be standing with you in prayers tonight for a testimony tomorrow morning. It does not take a tangent for God to change situations through miracles. God bless!

Secret Seven: Stop that separation and divorce, and move and make that reconciliation, using the instrument of influence.

HARRY TOBECHI NZE

Jista-Agapentine Family Support Network. P.O.box 844, Buckeye,Email: Jista.famagapentinenetwork@gmail.com

www.ingramcontent.com/pod-product-compliance
Lightning Source LLC
LaVergne TN
LVHW020434080526
838202LV00055B/5174